HOW TO BECOME A HAPPY WOMAN

BY Z. A. RICHARDS

Table of Contents.

Chapter 1-Who I Am and Why I Can Help You Become a Happy Woman

Chapter 2- The Causes of Unhappiness and How to Recognize Them.

Chapter 3- Why Men Make Women Unhappy

Chapter 4- Why Your Health Can Make You Unhappy

Chapter 5- Why Your Job Can Make You Unhappy.

Chapter 6-Who Are You?

WHO I AM AND WHY I CAN MAKE YOU BECOME A HAPPY WOMAN

First, full disclosure. I am not a licensed therapist, psychologist or medical professional of any kind.

I am also a man.

So why would I be qualified to instruct women on how to be happy? What does a guy know about a woman's happiness? Aren't all books on women's self-improvement and subsequent happiness written by women? Wouldn't they know best?

No. They don't.

Why? Because they're too close to the subject and are often not objective enough. They'll give feel good, clinical advice and follow all the therapeutic rules regarding happiness because most women want to be liked and appreciated. So do the women that write those books.

Me? As a man, I can give you insights you won't get from a woman. No touchy-feely, it's not your fault, hand holding nonsense. I'll give it to you straight so you can reach your goal of becoming a happy woman. But it's not going to be sunshine and lollipops. You'll likely discover personal flaws you didn't know you had. Character traits that might make you cringe. And realize that you've got to take action if you want to see results.

Because in those cases of where all is said and done… more is often *said,* than done.

By the time you finish reading this book you may hate my guts because what I'm going to tell you may seem insensitive. Or you may credit me with changing your life for the better. In either case, you'll know what to do to get yourself out of your slump and start becoming a happy and satisfied woman.

As for me, I'm a professional writer who was happily married for 25 years and together we raised two beautiful daughters who are now happy, successful adult women in their own right.

I wrote a very successful book titled *Divorce: The Middle-Aged Man's Survival Guide* because I knew a lot of men needed it. After decades of marriage, their wives simply decided they didn't want to be married anymore and that was that.

Their husbands were devastated. They thought everything was fine. There wasn't any big fight or infidelity or abuse. The men couldn't understand why they were abandoned.

After years of research, I discovered why and explained it to them. And once they understood, they were able to stop blaming themselves, stopped looking for reasons why their wives left and instead started building a new life.

Some wrote and told me my book probably saved their lives.

Happy to help.

When I noticed that a large number of women were dissatisfied and unhappy, I became curious as to the cause. I read several "how to be happy" books written by women, as well as some by supposedly knowledgeable female psychologists. And what struck me was the amount of hand holding, positive reinforcement and soothing compassion that flowed through the pages, **but nothing that actually addressed the problem, or provided solutions.**

Many women are unhappy because they are psychologically sabotaging themselves on a daily basis. They are unaware they are doing it and have no idea *why* they are doing it. Those subliminal acts are the central cause of their misery and that is what needs to be addressed and corrected. And by the time you finish reading this book, you'll know what is blocking you from becoming happy and what to do about it.

So let's get started.

One of the main stumbling blocks to a women's happiness lies in the unrealistic programming they received as children. Mostly created by well-meaning fathers who loved their daughters so much they couldn't let them pay for their mistakes. Couldn't stand to see them cry, couldn't bear to break their hearts.

And so they swooped in and made everything better. They told their daughters that when they did stupid things, it was all right. When they made bad choices, they were still loved and forgiven. And that it was acceptable to use their girlish charms or crocodile tears to get special consideration and favors without having to earn them.

The result? These girls grew into women who were programmed to believe that whenever they screwed up (men and woman do that equally) they need only go to the man in their lives and he will forgive them and do whatever is necessary to solve the problem.

Such programming (or lack thereof) doesn't permit her to exercise and strengthen her reasoning skills or develop a proper sense of accountability for her actions.

Basically, she remains a child in a woman's body. This leads to a difficult and often unhappy adulthood.

To avoid this happening to my daughters I treated them the same way I would treat my son. Example:

I had my daughter get a second job to pay for the damage she did to my car because she was texting while driving.

When they carelessly screwed up it often broke my heart to be so rigid, to ignore their tears, their pleas for forgiveness and instead insist they take action to correct their mistakes.

Yes, like every father I loved my daughters dearly (still do!) I wanted to take them into my arms and tell them I'd take care of it and that everything is going to be all right.

But I didn't.

Because I needed them to be prepared for how life REALLY works.

Because LIFE doesn't treat women any differently than men.

In the schoolyard, boys learn the hard way to steer clear of those who are bigger, stronger and prone to violence. Girls learn that boys are taught never to hit girls, and so never learn the real dangers of mouthing off to a guy prone to violence or how to spot them. (I made sure my daughters knew what to look for.)

Please note that I am in **no way** saying it's the woman's fault when a man physically abuses her.

Any man who strikes a woman is a bully and a coward. What I am saying is that a woman needs to acquire the same skills a man has when it comes to identifying and avoiding people who are prone to violence.

And this brings us to the bad boy syndrome.

There is a scene in the TV show the Big Bang Theory where Penny, the pretty female character bemoans the fact that all the guys she dates are cheating, misogynistic liars. "Why do I keep dating these guys?" she asks her two male friends, Sheldon and Leonard. "Am I just stupid?"

Without missing a beat, Sheldon replies, "Apparently."

Seeing Penny shocked and hurt by Sheldon's comment, Leonard immediately hugs and comforts her by reinforcing her belief that it's not her fault and that she's not responsible for her chain of disastrous relationships.

The problem here is yes, she is responsible. And yes, she is stupid to continue repeating behaviors she knows leads to misery. But it's not her fault because, throughout their lives, many women are programmed to desire dangerous and strong men. Men who don't obey the rules, who never back down from a fight, who tell their bosses to take this job and shove it. Guys who live life on their terms and don't take orders from anyone.

Bad Boys!

Here's the problem. Since bad boys don't obey society's rules, concepts of fidelity, honesty, responsibility, loyalty, chivalry, and respecting their fellow human beings are foreign to them.

This also leads to the woman becoming the abuser as in the "*guy friend*" scenario. This is where the girl is treated shabbily by her jock boyfriend and she unloads her troubles and woes to her guy friend who consoles her and tries to make her feel better.

A few days later, she gets a call from her boyfriend who says he's sorry, and without any consideration to the guy friend's feelings for her, blows him off and dashes off into the arms of her callous and mean boyfriend.

Shortly afterward she's back asking her guy friend why men are such insensitive bastards who have no consideration of how much they hurt another person's feelings.

Just once, in all the movies where this scenario is utilized I would like the guy friend to say, "Well, it's probably because that person is so focused on getting what *they* want and what makes *them* happy that they don't even realize the misery they are putting the other person through. Maybe they are so self-centered that they are oblivious to the fact that they are callous, and inconsiderate themselves.

The point is the girl is no less guilty of being a callous, self-centered jerk than the jock boyfriend. Both are only concerned with their own happiness and give little thought to anything else.

Dating is a process used to find the person you're going to marry. So I wouldn't allow my daughters to date until they were sixteen. The human brain isn't fully formed until age twenty-two, so dating before sixteen will likely do more harm than good.

When my daughter visits with her son, I am often stunned to hear her use, on her own child, the very same words and examples I used to raise her. When I asked her about it, she said that although she would never admit it at the time, I had a profoundly positive effect on her teen years. She said the lesson of the Stupid Chinese Man is the one that stuck with her the most.

It goes like this:

One afternoon my daughter came home from high school upset. I asked why, and she said some girls at school were calling her names and making fun of her. I let her tell her whole story, listening carefully.

When she finished, I said I had figured out what the problem was. She asked what, and I said, "It's because you're the stupidest, ugliest, Chinese man I have ever met."

Startled, she said, What?!! I'm not a stupid, ugly, Chinese man!"

Then I asked, "Do you think I'm intelligent?"

Nodding she said, "Yes, I think you're very intelligent.

So I replied, "So why would you believe those girls and not me?"

THE CAUSES OF UNHAPPINESS AND HOW TO RECOGNIZE THEM.

Believe it or not. You program your brain.

I'm serious. There is ample scientific proof that we program our brains. Meaning we become what we tell ourselves we are. I will qualify this fact by pointing out that mental illness is a physical disease and may play a serious part in people with self-destructive behaviors.

No amount of reprogramming is going to cure a physical illness.

If you suffer from clinical depression or have some of the symptoms that accompany it, then make an appointment with your doctor. The longer you put it off, the longer it will take for you to become happy again.

As for the rest of you, I'll give you an example of how it works. When a person consistently berates themselves with admonishments like "I'm such an idiot," or "I always screw things up" or "I never get anything right," you are literally programming your subconscious to make you appear as an idiot, to screw things up and to choose incorrect solutions. Without realizing it, those admonishments are causing your subconscious to take action to make you look bad.

I'll say it again so pay close attention. When you call yourself stupid, or a failure, or that you never do anything right, or any other admonishment that berates you, your subconscious will make you do things, or forget things or not see things that will cause you to look stupid or fail. This causes you to berate yourself more often, reinforcing that negative programming which in turn sabotages any chance of continued happiness.

This also occurs when someone consistently berates you and you don't demand they stop.

I'll give you an example that has likely happened to you. Someone asks you to go and get something. Say your spouse asks you to get the ketchup from the refrigerator. You go, look and don't see it, come back and say it's not there.

Your spouse replies "Of course it's in there. I put it there myself this morning. Please check again. You say, "I was just there. It's not in the refrigerator. I looked."

Spouse replies, "Please just look again, I'm sure it's there!"

You thunder off calling back, "I'm telling you, it's not there. I'm sure! I checked the entire refrigerator." You open the fridge, look again, still not there.

You spouse storms over, nudges you aside, and grabs the ketchup bottle that was right there on the top shelf. You feel like a fool and say to yourself, "I always screw things up."

Yes, you do. And the reason is because your subconscious is keeping you from seeing the ketchup, making you become the incompetent person you consistently tell yourself you are.

What you don't realize is that your brain screens what you see, only providing what it considers necessary information, because if you noticed everything, you wouldn't be able to walk and chew gum at the same time.

And when you program it by telling yourself you're defective, your subconscious will actively make you begin to behave that way. Ergo not seeing the ketchup.

Want to change your life? First, change yourself. And the way to do that is to change your self-programming. **Never, ever, berate yourself.** Instead, take a positive approach as in, *I'll get it right the next time*, or, *From now on I'm going to pay closer attention."*

Many people may view this as positive thinking, but positive thinking has major flaws. For example, you can tell yourself all day that there is a twenty-dollar bill in your pocketbook but, if you haven't put one there, no amount of positive thinking is going to put one there for you.

Instead, focus on positive **_goals_**. Plan on accomplishing one positive action today and refuse to go to bed until you accomplish it.

And write it down!

Writing things down reinforces our need to accomplish that act. It needn't be something big like washing all the window in the house. It could be as simple as sitting down and writing out a list of things that need to be done and the time afforded to accomplish them.

As in all things that are new, start small, accomplish your goals and then steadily increase them. The more you accomplish the more your self-esteem will increase. And it needn't be physical chores. A goal can be to read one book a month on a topic you're interested in. A goal could be to spend one day a month working at a soup kitchen or spend a half an hour a day for a month learning to play a musical instrument, or learning to quilt. Or create a vegetable garden.

And if you fail, so what!

The goal was to read a book a month. If you weren't able to accomplish that goal, write down why you weren't. And be honest. If it was because you really didn't want to make the effort to read that book, then say so and remove reading books from your list of goals, and focus on the others.

And should you fail to accomplish any of your goals, ask yourself why. And if the truthful answer was because you put it off, or never got around to it. Then the reason you are unhappy is because you aren't willing to do what needs to be done to become happy.

But what if you have a good excuse?

One of the most important things to understand in your quest to become a happy woman is that there is no such thing as an excuse, good or otherwise.

You either accomplish your goals or you don't.

Steve Jobs of Apple fame would often use this analogy when one of his product engineers would say something couldn't be improved or completed within a certain time frame. He would say to that engineer *If someone kidnapped your child and said they would kill him/her if you didn't improve a product or complete a certain task within a certain timeframe, might you be able to do it then?* Jobs would then shrug and say, *Think about it.*

In nearly every case the engineer would find a way to create that improvement or find a way to finish with a set time frame.

Most people naturally take the path of least resistance, It's in our nature. But if you want to be happy, then stop and have a closer look at your actions. Do you put things off and then forget to do them and have to double your effort at a later date or pay more than you intended to?

If this is the case, then it is a partial cause of your unhappiness. I had this flaw and was beating myself up because of it.

But what good did that do? Did it solve the problem? No. Was I properly punished for that behavior? Apparently not because I continued to do it, and more often because I was telling myself I was lazy and disorganized.

Then I decided to DO something about it. I bought a small notepad and kept it in my back pocket. Then whenever I needed to do something or tend to something I would write it down so I wouldn't forget it.

Now I just use my phone scheduler to remind me.

We are all human and we all make mistakes. Mistakes are how we learn. Say, for example, you spend hours working on a project on your computer, then are distracted by some ad.

Curious, you click on the ad without saving your work. You come back and discover that all your work is gone! Frustrated, you're about to call yourself all sorts of abusive names.

Remember, your subconscious is listening and eager to help you become what you say you are.

This is not to say you can't be angry or frustrated. By all means rail at cruel fate, bad software, and evil marketers who distract you with shiny things.

Just don't attack yourself.

The Difference Between a Must and a Should.

I regularly read, listen and watch people like Tony Robbins, Zig Ziglar, Jim Rhon, Robert Kiyosaki, Jim Kern, Ray Dalio and a number of others who have mastered certain skills in life and were kind enough to bring them before the public in the forms of books, audios, and videos.

I could kick myself for not following them earlier but I either didn't know they existed or had a mistaken opinion of who they were and what they did.

Case in point, Tony Robbins.

Tony Robbins is what is presently called a life coach. I have become a real fan because the training he gives has proven to be so valuable. And what particularly struck me was his training on the difference between a should and a must.

He says that the reason most people fail to achieve what they want is because of their attitude regarding should and must.

For example, some people say to themselves, I *should* lose weight. And they make an attempt at first but it usually peters out after a few weeks or days.

But if your doctor tells you that your kidneys are failing and in order to be eligible for a kidney transplant, you must lose 60 pounds. At this point *should* no longer figures into it.

What we have now is a ***must.***

And that is how you MUST approach your goals. You no longer *should* become a happy woman. You *must* become a happy woman and will do whatever it takes regardless of the time, effort or sacrifices required

Why? Because it is now a MUST!

If you intend to succeed in becoming happy, one of the more important changes to make is learning to only choose projects that you must complete. Too often people (not just women) fall into the bad habit of starting a project and then lose their enthusiasm and the project is abandoned.

What you are doing is creating failures that continue to add up. And when you look back on the year, you realize that you attempted a number of things but didn't accomplish any of them. It is better emotionally and psychologically to not begin a project than to start one and not complete it.

So going back to where we spoke of taking the time to self-analyze, and search for patterns in your behavior. Is starting a project and not finishing it something you always do? Something you occasionally do, or something you never do?

Sometimes all three apply, if that is the case, categorize those projects into failures and successes. In most cases a pattern will emerge. For example, say you've attempted to learn a foreign language on several occasions but just couldn't stick with it long enough to be able to communicate with a person who was fluent.

What this is telling you is that learning a foreign language is not a must. It's barely even a should. It just seemed like a good idea at the time. And what seemed like a good idea did nothing but waste your valuable time.

Then look at the successes. I'm going to pause here to explain the success choices I will be using as examples are stereotypically those of women. I fully understand and believe that women can be as skilled as any man in whatever field they choose. But I'm going with those stereotypical choices because they are more associated with women than men.

And with that being said, say the projects you did accomplish were the ones that were artistic and required creativity. You learned the art of pottery making, or flower arraigning, or quilting, or dress making, or interior design, or house repair.

Yes, house repair. Although usually associated with men (Note, there aren't any women on Ask This Old House) my sister and a female writer friend of mine are both very skilled at home repair.

As mentioned earlier, I'm not. I no longer attempt home repair and improvement projects. Because when I did, they quickly became disasters and drove me into a rage. Fortunately, my sister is very calm and clear headed so I turn those projects over to her and she does an excellent job every time.

What I AM good at regarding home improvement is in the design. I had an old pool removed from by backyard and designed a new deck and barbecue pit to replace it. I simply drew what I wanted it to look like and the tradespeople used their talents and skills to bring my design to fruition.

Over the years, I've made several improvements to my home by designing what I wanted done and having qualified people build to my specifications.

Increase your knowledge and skills with projects you will finish. Don't waste valuable time trying the master skills you simply don't have the talent for. Sure, I'd love to be able to actually build the projects I've designed, but I've learned not to because it is simply a waste of time.

MAKE EVERY PROJECT A MUST.

Don't waste time and energy trying to become something you're not. The older you get the more you will realize how important your time is. And the more time you have to do the things you want to do, the happier you will be.

Conversely, the more time you spend doing things you have no talent or interest in, the more unhappier you will be.

One of the differences between a sad person and a happy person is a happy person LEARNS from the mistake. They take action not to repeat their mistake and close the loop on their self-destructive behavior.

As a writer, I would often spend hours writing copy only to be distracted by some pop-up and make the mistake of clicking on it then realizing the ramifications of what I'd done.

So to remedy this behavior I had a mouse pad created that said in huge red letters

STOP

Have you saved your work!!??

That solved the problem.

The takeaway is this. In order to become a happy woman, you will need to change the behavior that leads to unhappiness.

And this will require determination and perseverance on your part. And I won't be asking you to do things I haven't done myself.

When I was downsized during the financial meltdown, like many people, I couldn't get a job. So I started looking for ways to improve myself to appear more attractive to the job market.

And by doing so, I discovered the more I changed and improved my behavior, the better my life became.

So let's take a moment to review.

You have become what you were programmed to be. If you are unhappy it's because you were programmed, either by yourself or by others to do things that lead to unhappiness.

So let's start with a self-appraisal. To do this you need to be by yourself. You need to concentrate and most importantly, to be completely honest.

And this may be difficult because women hate to be viewed as the bad guy, but as human beings, we all have things we regret having done. And that's the first goal. Accept that you are human and have made mistakes.

And one of the biggest mistakes we all make is forgiving ourselves for our errors **before** changing ourselves to make sure we don't make those mistakes again.

Saying you're sorry doesn't absolve you, nor does it correct the mistake. Only by taking action to undo it, do you learn and grow as a person.

In addition, you may feel that the source of your unhappiness is your mate's fault. That may be and if so, you already know what you need to do to make yourself happy. But remember. We are not here to point out men's mistakes. They make their share, but the goal here is to make <u>*you*</u> happy, and you will not become happy by focusing on their shortcomings. Because if your happiness depends on the actions of someone else then your happiness is out of your control. And to paraphrase Martha Stewart, "That's a bad thing."

So what are the traits of happy women?

Not surprisingly, they are very similar to that of men. The first thing we need as human beings to be happy is security. Note that we're not talking just about money, although money can be an important factor. The security I'm talking about is personal security

Do you feel safe in your environment, in your personal relationships, with your finances, with your job? If not, that's where you start.

It's impossible to be happy if you're constantly on edge, worrying about your security issues. Do you live in a dangerous neighborhood? Do you feel threatened by your husband, boyfriend or significant other? Is your job environment hostile, coworkers difficult or boss unreasonable? Have you been ostracized by family or friends?

If any of those issues apply to you, it's time to create an action plan. Later in this book I'll tell you what actions to take to improve your situation.

The next thing you'll need is to discover is the meaning of your life. What makes you unique?

What makes you an individual? We are all unique in our own way and valuable regarding our own talents.

These days most people view famous people as important. People like rock stars, movie stars, sports stars and so on.

But what if there was a major catastrophe? Say the government collapsed, food was scarce, no gasoline, the internet no longer functioned, and paper money no longer had value?

Who would be important then? Certainly not the rock stars and the like. The most important people would be those who could get food to people, those who knew how to hunt, how to grow food and what wild food could be eaten. How to build shelter, how to mend clothes.

People need to remember that although your particular skills aren't very important right now, it doesn't mean they won't be very important in the future.

So what you need to focus on is personal growth. Many people make the mistake of thinking that once they have enough money to retire they will live happily ever after, relaxing in the sun and puttering around the house.

No, they won't. Why? Because we need to keep developing ourselves, because personal growth leads to happiness and personal fulfillment.

Like every living thing, if you're not growing… you're dying.

And in order to achieve happiness, you must become the person you were meant to be. I'll give you an example.

For decades, I worked in corporate. I made good money. My bosses, for the most part, were experienced and professional and I got along well with my co-workers. Most people would be very happy in such an environment.

But I was miserable.

Why? Because I was spending my life doing tasks I had absolutely no interest in. I'm a night person yet I had to get up at 6 am Monday through Friday, then work from eight to five. I had to wear a suit, which I find restrictive and uncomfortable. I don't get hungry until around 3 in the afternoon, but my lunch hour was scheduled for Noon.

Basically, everything I was doing was contrary to my natural inclinations. Fortunately, that's not the case anymore. The change came during my excursion into personal development.

As I was listening to an audiobook on self-improvement the author asked, *"What job would you do even if you weren't getting paid for it?"*

That is probably the most important question you will ever ask yourself.

Why? Because the answer will help you discover the person you are supposed to be and the job you are supposed to do. And believe me, the most fulfilling and joy creating moments in your life are those spent doing the things you were born to do.

The better part of my life was spent doing business math and calculations, profit and loss, credit and finance. It was a skill I acquired because it was needed for me to advance in the marketplace.

You see, my programming, like those of many of my generation, was to get a good education so we could get a good job. No other options were to be considered. Hopes and aspirations? That was daydreaming, and people who daydreamed never amounted to anything.

So I followed my programming, did what I had to do. Supported my family, bought a house and sent my kids to college so they could get a good education so they could get a good job and so the circle of life could continue.

Then the meltdown of 2008 hit, and all the accepted rules became obsolete.

So what was my answer to the author's question of what job would I do even if I didn't get paid?

I gave that A LOT of thought. I knew I had to be honest and, after considerable soul searching, here's what I came up with.

I realized I was, at heart, a creative person. When I was a kid I used to write and draw my own comic books. As I got older I would design logos for local rock bands, I was a problem solver, I was self-disciplined and a self-starter. Then I realized I was not at all comfortable taking orders and doing what other people told me to do, regardless of the amount of money they were paying.

So what job would I do even if I didn't get paid for it?

My answer? I would run my own business.

Frankly that conclusion startled me. I had never considered opening my own business. Growing up we were never taught how to do that. We were taught that we work for other people, people didn't work for us.

I asked myself, ***What makes me think I could build a successful business?*** Then I thought, ***What makes me think I can't?***

My mind immediately started coming up with excuses. Why I couldn't, why I shouldn't, why I wouldn't.

Still, the idea resonated with me. I liked the idea of being my own boss.

Then I realized I didn't want to be a merchant. Not that I have anything against them. Having my own business taught me just how difficult being a successful merchant is. I simply wasn't interested in buying something wholesale and selling it retail.

I wanted to create my own products and sell them.

And so I realized that's the goal I needed to accomplish.

And so I did. HOW I did it will be discussed later in the job chapter.

WHY MONEY CAN MAKE YOU UNHAPPY

The next thing you will need to become a happy woman is to acquire financial security.

Too many of us spend our lives like a hamster on a spinning wheel. We go to work, collect our pay, then take care of the bills and hopefully have enough left over to put something aside in our saving account.

That behavior leads to a financial death spiral. Why? Because there are four quadrants of taxation.

- **Employees:** People who work for a company pay the most in taxes. Their 401k saving plan places your money in the hands of financial managers who invest that money in projects or stocks they believe will generate a profit. What you likely don't know is that those financial managers invest your money in ventures that will benefit them first, not you. They get paid whether those ventures generate a profit with your money or not. These people take no personal nor financial risk and so they often exceed reasonable risk to increase their profits. Your expectations are rarely considered. This behavior is what led to the 2008 financial meltdown.
- **Self- Employed**, people who have their own business, doctors, lawyers, merchants etc.

This group is the second most heavily taxed. Because they make more money and tend to keep a watchful eye on their investments they often do better than employees tax wise. Because they have a say in where their money is invested, they're likely to it placed in ventures that have a lower tax rate.

- **Big Business**, companies with more than 500 employees. These companies often pay a much lower percentage than the two previous tax quadrants because they generate more taxpayers, ie. construction of their facility, use of utilities, purchasing of business machines and furniture, and taxes from employees.
- **Investors.** These people pay little and often no taxes because they take the money collected in 401Ks and pension plans and, with other investors, place that money in a capital venture like building apartment houses, or strip malls, or financing new businesses, or for oil drilling, and gold mining.

These are the risk takers, the ones who stick their noses out, using their money combined with yours to fuel the economy, create jobs and curb inflation. These people know how business works far better than you. For example; Robert Kiyosaki of **Rich Dad, Poor Dad** fame predicted the 2008 meltdown with considerable accuracy, and nearly a decade before it happened. He wrote two other books with Donald Trump titled, *Why We Want You to Be Rich* and *Midas Touch*.

Remember what we told you about the necessity of having security in your life? One very good method is to start reading and learning about investing and finance. It's not a boring as you might expect and it's relatively inexpensive to do. You can start with as little as twenty dollars and when you see your first profit, that will bring a smile to your face.

Tony Robbins wrote a best-selling book titled ***MONEY Master the Game***. In it, he shows you exactly how to invest, what to invest in and how to make a profit with your investments each and every time.

So if your finances are the reason you're not happy or fulfilled, you should get a copy of Tony's book and learn how to end your financial problems.

However, if you have spending problems and simply can't properly manage your finances, then you need to hire a money manager. A money manager is someone who will handle all your bills for you, see that all the necessary expenses are taken care of and then turn over the rest to you.

For an agreed upon fee of course.

I know a few women who have found this to be a Godsend. Everyone has flaws and weaknesses. And one of the best ways to become happy is to find out what these flaws are and then take action to eliminate them. A woman I know had a real problem with buying shoes. So much so that she almost maxed out her credit card.

Fortunately, she saw that she had a problem, hired a money manager who, over a period of time was able to make her debt free.

And yes, she still buys shoes but only with the money allotted to her after all her expenses are taken care of. But surprisingly, she doesn't have the same obsession anymore. Apparently it was the mounting debt brought about by buying shoes that fueled her anxiety, which led her to buy even more shoes to ease that anxiety.

Personally, although she hadn't told me so, I believe that the cause of her problem sprang from her admonishing herself each time she spent money on shoes. And the more she admonished herself the more her subconscious would lead her to believe that buying those shoes would make her happy.

And it would, for a short time.

Then the admonishments would begin and the cycle would repeat itself. I also believe that she instinctively berated herself because as a child, when she did, her father, or father figure would tell her she wasn't to blame and would solve the problem for her.

If you want to understand how money really works and why some people with just a few dollars' investment become millionaires while the great majority do not, then watch this 30-minute video and learn what the rich people know and the regular people do not.

http://www.economicprinciples.org/

One of the major causes of unhappiness is money troubles. This single issue has led to the end of the majority of marriages. One of the most important questions to ask a potential mate is their views on money.

Differences of opinion on this issue can be a deal breaker when it comes to impending nuptials and it should be. Although you may have differences in political opinions, religion, where to live, how to raise the children or any number of things, you and your spouse's views on money and how it is to be spent must be as similar as possible.

Here's why. If both spouses agree on a certain investment and that investment goes sour, they both knew and accepted the possibility of failure and simply mark it up to experience.

On the other hand, if one spouse opposes investing their money in stocks or real estate and the other staunchly insists that it is the opportunity of a lifetime. There will be trouble regardless of who is right.

If the investment generates income and security, the one opposed will resent it. If it tanks, the one who insisted upon it will be subjected to an onslaught of "I told you so."

If the core of your unhappiness is due to poor management of your money, then start devoting your free time to learning how to increase your income and generate more income with that knowledge.

Imagine the freedom you will feel when you don't need to concern yourself about money or where your next dollar is coming from.

WHY YOUR HEALTH CAN MAKE YOU UNHAPPY

Your next goal is to acquire **Personal Health**.

When a person allows themselves to become sad or depressed it has a considerable effect on their health. Remember you become what you tell yourself you are. And because of that, you can put yourself in serious physical jeopardy by telling yourself you feel lousy because life is giving you a hard time.

Do that consistently and your subconscious will create psychosomatic aches and pains which can lead to thinking that you have a serious disease like cancer or heart disease. Such thinking will only add to the anxiety which subsequently will only bring about more discomfort.

The bottom line is that your potential happiness depends on _**your**_ choices. Choose to improve your life by learning to do the things you were born to do and you will be stunned by the rewards it brings.

Choose to do nothing and nothing will improve. And this is dangerous. And more dangerous than most people believe when it comes to your health.

Most of the psychologically destructive programming we receive is from the media.

They feature exceptionally beautiful people as clothes models for average looking people. Exceptionally talented athletes telling you that you can have the type of body they have. Exceptionally wealthy entrepreneurs telling you to get out there and make money like they did.

This is disheartening because the majority of us aren't exceptional, yet exceptional is featured as the norm. This makes us feel inferior so we buy what they're selling and when it doesn't do for us (make us attractive, strong or rich) what it did for them, we often fall into depression and self-destructive behaviors.

Remember, things don't lead to happiness. They often bring temporary joy and upbeat feelings but those feelings don't last. For example, most of my life I drove cheap compact cars because with a family and the expenses that come with it, that was all I could afford.

Once I started making some real money with my business I bought a BMW. To me, owning a BMW was always the pinnacle of success. And it is everything they claim it to be. An absolutely beautiful, enjoyable and comfortable ride.

The thing is after a month or so, I found myself driving my 15-year-old Hyundai once again. It used less gas, didn't require me to look the part of a BMW driver. (Seriously, you just can't drive a BMW wearing a faded T-shirt and sweatpants) which is what I normally wear since I work in my home office. And I didn't have to worry about spilling coffee, or staining the carpets with dropped food.

Still love the BMW but now I only drive it when I'm going to meet with clients or am attending a business meeting.

Woe is Me

Hard times are a fact of life. And those struggles can leave emotional scars that will need to be addressed psychologically in order to heal. Too often people tend to compensate by overeating, drinking alcohol, sexual promiscuity, and other bad habits that become vices that will continue to plague you long after the hard times are over.

During a particularly difficult time in my life, I became depressed and began living off junk food. I ate only what I liked and virtually nothing healthful. I don't think I ate a green vegetable or a piece of fruit in 2 straight years.

As a result, I became fat and out of shape. I also developed a number of health problems. Ulcers, shortness of breath, constant heartburn, swollen wrists and ankles, high blood pressure, sleep apnea and others.

Then God showed up in the form of an infomercial.

I was laying on the couch stuffing my face with some form of sugary crap when Dr. Joel Fuhrman appeared on the screen and said, "The reason you are fat, unhealthy and constantly hungry is because you are not eating the foods your body needs to properly function. And since you are not eating those foods, your brain is constantly sending out hunger signals in the hope that you will finally eat the foods it actually needs."

To me, that made perfect sense. So I stopped eating and started listening.

He talked about his book titled, **Eat to Live**. In it, he explained why your body needs to eat certain foods each day and if you ate them, your brain would stop making you hungry and therefore you would naturally eat less and lose weight.

But what really sold me was when he said that by eating those foods, most, if not all, of the ailments I was presently suffering from due to my unhealthy diet would be cured.

Normally I'm a hard sell. It takes a lot for me to reach for my wallet. But everything he said during that infomercial rang true to me. So I ordered a copy.

When I received it, I read it and the more I read, the more sense it made. So I began eating the foods he said I needed (Although I didn't cut out red meat, I'm a carnivore and there is no changing that.) Nevertheless, over a period of three months I lost 38 pounds and all my physical ailments vanished.

That was my first realization that by me taking action and changing myself, I could change my life. And that's the point I will keep reinforcing throughout this book. When I saw the dramatic effect Dr. Fuhrman's diet plan had on me, I realized that there were likely hundreds of other things I could learn to make my life better, happier and more fulfilling.

If you have health and/or weight issues I highly recommend reading his book. But even if you don't, I will tell you the foods your body needs the function properly anyway, and that you will need to eat them in some form each day for optimum results.

Dr. Fuhrman calls it the GOMBS diet. GOMBS stand for Greens, Onions, Mushrooms, Berries and Seeds/nuts.

Here's an example of what I eat. In the morning I'd have blueberry or strawberry yogurt with a teaspoon of ground flax seeds (flax seeds have no taste) then for lunch I'd have a hamburger with mushrooms and onions and for dinner, chicken with green beans, potatoes, and a salad. I also began a low impact exercise regimen because as my health improved, I had more energy so I put it to good use.

Any combination of those five foods during the day will do the trick. In addition, the book contains a large number of recipes that can spice things up as well as other health-producing foods like beans, kiwis and avocados.

Taking action to become healthy will have a huge effect on your mood, energy, and well-being. There is no reason for you to suffer. But nothing will change unless you do. And a simple adjustment to your diet now may prevent serious and life-threatening conditions in the future.

Avoid Negative People

There is one behavior that no amount of good health or financial security will benefit. And that is the addiction to the endorphins that come with being the victim. The martyr, the sacrificer. That's a difficult habit to break and it's common in many women.

Women are, for the most part, nurturers. They want to help, they want to take care of those they love, they want to be needed and appreciated.

But…

If those needs are not fulfilled through normal means, an addiction to the endorphins that come with being the center of attention can lead to a very self-destructive mindset.

You've likely have come in contact with one of these women. The one that stays with the abusive husband, the one who lives in squalor because her husband's a drunk and she has to work two jobs. Or the one with the wild and uncontrolled children or any number of tragedies she feels she is forced to endure.

You offer solutions but she never follows through. She has numerous excuses why your solutions won't work for her or why they didn't work when she supposedly tried them.

The reason is that she is an addict. She feels an enormous rush when someone listens to her continuing tales of woe. Of her hardships and the sacrifices she's had to make.

Do your best to avoid these people. And if you have to interact with them, don't feed their addiction. If she tries to force her problems on you, reply with, "I'm sorry but I'm a positive person and your unfortunate situation is something I have no control over so I would prefer not to hear any more about it."

Please note that this does not apply to someone who is suffering from a sudden loss or life-altering tragedy. By all means do what you can to comfort that person. We are all here to help one another, we are *not* here, however, to be someone crutch or wailing wall.

Your primary responsibility is to readjust your life so that you wake up to a day filled with promise and possibilities. You will have to endure your share of difficulties, that's life and sometimes there is little or nothing we can do about things like your house burning down or someone stealing your car.

On the other hand, happy people don't take foolish risks. They take the time to make sure the insurance coverage they have covered all their needs. Because when you're dealing with a business, it's their goal to give you as little as possible for as much as the market will allow. So it is wise to check your policies regularly to make sure you're **actually covered** for what you believe you're covered for.

So we have addressed personal growth and personal finances.

Next, it's time to address **Your Personality**.

Let's start with mine.

For the better part of my life, I have been disliked by my peers. They never came right out and said so but it became obvious when I would get into a disagreement with someone and my so-called friends would take my opponents side every time.

It's been said that as you approach the latter part of your life God shows you why you lived the life you lived and most importantly, why you got what you deserved.

As for me, yeah, I deserved it. And the reason I deserved it is because I was graced with a number of special talents, a quick wit, and relatively good looks. But what God gives with one hand HE often takes with the other.

My personality, for example, was similar to that of a chimpanzee with a machine gun. I did not possess that filter that most people have that prevents them from saying whatever stupid and often cruel thing that pops into their head and, coupled with the talents that I often displayed thinking I was entertaining people, got me labeled as a smart-mouthed, show off.

And looking back, I was. Not intentionally, but I can see now that showing all I could do to people who didn't have comparable abilities was just asking for trouble.

So I spent the better part of my youth getting into fights and getting detention at school. I became the stereotypical angry youth with a chip on his shoulder.

What I really needed was for someone to sit me down and explain why my actions were counter-productive and what I needed to do to change them. But it's likely someone or a number of somebodies did. And thinking it was a personal attack, I verbally sliced them to ribbons.

Which was something I had become VERY good at.

Although I mellowed with age I still didn't understand my problem nor how to control it. It wasn't until I was downsized and got into self-improvement education that my personality issues came into focus and I took action to correct them.

And no, it wasn't easy to change and it took a considerable amount of time to curb my tongue and become the easy going, affable, friend and neighbor I am today.

If they only knew…

Now the time has come to look at yourself. There is an old saying that goes: *If we could only see ourselves as others see us.*

One of the great boosts to happiness and fulfillment is to have friends and attend social gatherings. So how many friends do you have? A lot of close and long term, some close and long term, few close and long term…

None?

Your friends should mirror who you are. I used to have just one close friend now I have many with the list continuing to grow and ebb. The reason for this is we need certain people in our lives at certain times. But as those times pass, those friendships wither and new ones are formed.

So where do you find these people?

If you want to grow socially you need to first do a personal assessment of who you are, what traits you possess, what interests you have, and an understanding of your social cell.

Your social cell are the people who have traits and interests similar to yours. For example, when I needed to make new friends I decided to frequent a local sports bar because it had a friendly atmosphere, the food was good and everyone seemed to get along.

But it didn't take long until I realized that I didn't fit in because these people weren't members of my social group. These people were sports fans, tradesmen, and government employees. Good, friendly people but I didn't fit in.

I'm not a sports fan, have no idea what March madness is, I watch the Superbowl for the commercials. I have no idea how to repair an automobile, build a bookcase or repair a leaky sink or faucet.

What I can do is play eight musical instruments, I've written 15 books, I won the Writers Voice Award with my first novel, I design business logos, create business videos, construct business sales pages, build websites, and publish books. I also own several businesses and only work when the mood suits me.

Ergo the smart-mouthed show-off. But I think you can see why that sports bar wasn't a good fit. So I decided to redirect my focus.

Which is what you need to do. Go back to the question of what job would you do even if you weren't getting paid, because it also provides a good idea of who is in your social cell.

And once you have a good idea of what you are, what you do is join a group of like-minded people. For example, sign up for night classes in the discipline you're interested in. Take something of general interest, like cooking. Join a cooking class or if you're interested in quilting, join a quilting bee. Or computer programming, well you get the picture.

When I decided I needed to make more friends I went to open mike cafes and played piano, made a few friends there, then I joined a writers' group and made more. Then one of my new friends invited me to a restaurant to have a few drinks. Turned out this restaurant's clientele were professional people discussing business. There were no big screen TVs featuring sports, sports and more sports. Just easy-listening music in the background which is conducive to conversation and interacting with new people.

I had found my social cell.

Now you need to go and find yours.

WHY MEN MAKE WOMEN UNHAPPY

Poor Choices in Relationships.

As mentioned earlier, I read a number of self-improvement books designed to help women. And found them to be overwhelmingly centered on dealing with men. How to deal with a jerk, with a cheater, with a this or a that.

According to these books, women are obsessed with the problems they have with men and the need to solve them.

Here's what you need to understand. The problem isn't with men.

The problem is that women choose with their heart instead of their head.

I am going answer to your questions about why men are the way they are, and it's not the answer you'll want to hear. That why my method of teaching you to become a happier woman is better than the advice you get from women authors.

So let's begin.

There is an old and very true saying. And it goes like this.

A woman marries a man thinking he will change, but he doesn't. A man marries a woman thinking she won't change, but she does.

I don't usually teach using old time platitudes but the saying does point out a very common error women make. And that error is thinking that if he loves her enough, he will change.

No, he won't. Oh sure, because he loves her he will make an effort, but eventually, he will go back to his old ways because that's who he is.

I'll give you an example. How often have you seen tabloids stories of super athletes getting caught cheating on their wives?

Happens all the time. And everyone feels sorry for the wife, she's the victim, the poor, loyal, wonderful wife.

She's no victim. She knew exactly what she was getting into. How could she not? Her husband is a virtual superman. The perfect body, the perfect face, the perfect everything. He's a massive success in his sport. The temptations of the flesh are available to him 24/7 All free, no questions asked.

And because he is the perfect specimen, nature wants him to procreate as much as possible. His sex drive is insatiable. The pheromones his body gives off attracts women of all kinds because subconsciously women want to breed with superior, powerful males.

She saw how all the women were attracted to him and because women are so competitive with each other, she set her sights on winning him for herself.

And she did. Now she expects this powerful young stallion to settle down and become a plow horse.

Really!!??

Frankly that is downright unrealistic, delusional and extremely egotistical on that woman's part. It is a massive rush to her feminine ego to believe that this attractive and powerful man will be with only her for the rest of his life, and so she ignores the logistics and realities involved.

And this is where a woman's heart betrays her head.

Only a fool believes he could magically transform himself into something that is the complete opposite of what he is. That he would live the life of Clark Kent instead of Superman because she wants him to.

However, the woman who chooses with her head understands and has come to terms with her situation.

Yes, she'll get the mansion, the fancy cars, the yacht, the last name that gives her instant access to whatever she wants. And all the perks that come with marrying a superior man.

And she'll likely have the life she envisioned for herself since childhood.

But the woman who chooses with her head knows these things come with a price. Every woman wants him, every woman will do whatever is in her power to seduce him, to lure him away from you and put themselves in your place.

So the woman who chooses with her head will look the other way and ignore the occasional dalliances because no one gets everything they want in life. And because she's got far more than most and took the time to understand and accept what she was getting into, has no intention of making an issue of something she has no control over.

If you want an example of how this works just look at Bill and Hilary Clinton. They knew each other since college. And she's no fool. She saw that Bill was a womanizer from the very beginning, but she also realized that this was a man who was going places. This was a man who was destined to be a major player in life.

And she wanted in on that.

And what did looking the other way get her?

How about being one of the most powerful and influential women in existence.

And to an ambitious and success driven woman like Ms. Clinton, it seemed like a fair trade.

Now I'm not condoning infidelity. In fact I'm very much against it. But I am often stunned when women walk blindly into relationships when the guys has already shown himself to be prone to violence, or a womanizer, or a heavy drinker, or a liar, or gambler. And then act as if she's a victim!

So let me make this very clear. If you marry a man prone to violence, you will become a battered wife. If you marry a womanizer, you will be cheated on, a liar, you will be lied to, and so on...

That WILL happen.

If you want to be a happy woman then forget the fairy tales and romanticism and place a hard focus on the realities.

Men are not hard-wired to be romantic. We are very basic. We are looking for a woman we can be ourselves with. And when we we come in contact one who might fit that criteria we will make some stumbling, half-assed attempt to get to know her better.

You need to know that real guys are inexperienced in meeting women. They need to summon all their courage because they've been callously shot down before. The stuff you see in movies and read in books are created to be exactly what women want because it sells. Not because it happens.

And when you meet a man who is smooth and romantic, says all the right things and sweeps you off your feet, you need to ask yourself, HOW DID HE GET THAT WAY?

It's because he's had a lot of practice with a lot of women. So don't be surprised when your girlfriend tells you that he hit on her behind your back.

Want the keys to the kingdom when it comes to dating the man you want? It's amazingly simple.

First find out all you can about him. Just to make sure the guy isn't a potential problem. Then go up to him and ask a question that leads to a converation.

It could be something as simple as, "Do you have the time," and point to your wrist. When he answers thank him and compliment something about him. Like "That's a nice jacket. Or "That's a nice cellphone, where did you get it?"

Then here's the closer. Have a business card made and say,"You seem nice and I enjoyed talking to you, if you'd like to talk again call me, here's my card and hand it to him.

It doesn't matter what it says. It could be Sally Smith custom cakes. Or real estate, or whatever. And if he asks about it say you don't do that anymore but the number is good.

Then smile and walk away. He'll either call or he won't. In any case you've taken positive action to get what you want. To acquire something you feel may make you happy.

Maybe it will and maybe it won't but what's important is you've begun to take control. You're making things happen FOR you, not letting thing happen TO you.

As I said earlier, everything has changed. There is nothing unladylike when it comes to getting what you want. Once you decide to see life as it really is and not the romanticised version, you're on your way to becoming a happy woman.

Another amazing example of skewed thinking is the breakup of the Sandra Bullock/Jesse James marriage. Of course, Sandra is the victim but let's look at the whole story.

During their marriage, Sandra made a movie titled **The Proposal**. It was a romantic comedy in which she appears not only completely nude but on top of an also completely nude Ryan Reynolds.

On a talk show while doing promotion of the film, she mentioned that the scene was filmed from a number of different angles causing *"her lady parts to smack him in the face and for his guy parts to do the same to her."* She laughed and added that if the movie does well, maybe she's do all her movies in the nude.

Everybody laughed, all great fun.

You can bet her husband, Jesse James, a mountain of testosterone and the ultimate example of the proverbial Bad Boy wasn't laughing. There was his wife, naked on top of another man, for everyone to see.

Apparently Sandra hadn't given any thought as to how her husband would react to her "I'll show you mine if you show me yours," romp on the screen.

So he got naked and got on top of another naked woman. Only his sexual antics weren't shown in movie houses around the country.

Still he's condemned as a home wrecker and cheater while she still remains America's Sweetheart.

The core problem with their relationship is that they obviously didn't create their set of marriage rules.

If, before they got married, she said, "Jesse, I'm an actress and actresses are often required to do love scenes in the nude, I just want you to understand that before we get married." And if he said, "I understand but as a powerful and highly sexual male, I going to need to step outside the marriage occasionally for a little action on the side. I just wanted you to understand that before we got married."

If both had accepted those conditions, there never would have been a problem.

You see, the error here is this new feministic idea that as a woman she can do whatever she wants without consequences and that no man has the right to tell her she can't.

And I agree with that. Until you get married. Once you're married you have formed a partnership, you are now part of a team. What should be foremost in your mind (and his) is how will your actions affect your relationship? If it can damage it, even if only slightly, don't do it. Not because he told you not to, but because you both agreed to the rules and as responsible adults, you live your life in accordance with them.

If you discover that a male friend or co-worker is becoming attracted to you and you aren't taking action to avoid interacting with that person, that's a perfect example of making a bad choice. Because although it can provide some harmless, temporary happiness, and maybe some much-needed attention, that innocent flirtation too often stops being harmless and leads to misery, broken marriages and the loss of trust from your children and family.

***

If you intend to become happy, you must analyze any possible relationship with your head, NOT YOUR HEART.

Yes, I believe in romance and love and two people being made for each other. But it is absolutely imperative that you accept the package you're buying into. You simply cannot reasonably expect a man to act in a manner that is contrary to what he was genetically built to do.

If you fall in love with a sweet, loving nerd, don't expect him to start throwing punches whenever some guy hits on you. Don't expect an electrical engineer to write you love sonnets and send flowers. Don't expect an avid outdoorsman to become a homebody. And don't expect a CPA to become an extroverted life of the party.

If you marry a duck, don't expect to ride it like a horse. Or your duck to change into a horse because he loves you. That's unrealistic, egocentric and completely unfair.

And here's the MOST important question you need to ask yourself BEFORE you become seriously involved, and one you must answer totally truthfully.

Think back to when you were a child and imagine that the man your mother married is the guy you're planning on settling down with. If he became YOUR dad, how good a relationship would that be? Would he be a good dad? Would he be there when you needed him?

Now take a moment to think of your potential daughter. Would she be terrified of him? Would he order her around, make her his personal servant, berate her, slap her, yell at her?

Remember, your child will be the spitting image of you, possessing much of the same personality and fears you have.

If you recoil at the thought of him being YOUR father, then why would you subject your child to him?

Also, pay attention to how he treats those in the service industry. Is he rude to waiters and waitresses, or salesclerks? How does he treat pets and animals?

Sometimes it difficult to tell the difference between a strong man and a bully.

And don't delude yourself into thinking you can change him or that it will be different when you are married.

It won't.

It will get worse.

***

So how do you wind up with the completely wrong guy.?

You choose him and deluded yourself into thinking that he'll change and become the person you imagine him to be.

And why do some women expect that to happen? It's because as a girl they cried, pleaded, pouted, stomped their foot, pulled a snit, stormed around the house and generally made life miserable until she got what she wanted. And so she's programmed herself into thinking those actions provide results and by using them she will attain the goals she's set for herself.

They will not, however, change a duck into a horse. When it doesn't she will be enormously disappointed, heartbroken and unable to understand why he is so mean to her.

And that happens! There are some women who actually believe that he is intentionally refusing to become what she wants him to be, out of spite.

Unfortunately, it will not occur to her that she may have made the wrong choice.

Here's a common example.

Several of your ten girlfriends tell you he's not right for you. The others are either non-committal or have nothing good to say about him. You defend him by saying they can't see the special qualities and sensitivities he shows only to you. You know him better than they do. And you're determined to convince them you made the right choice.

That's so romantic and touching but here's the question you need to ask yourself,

*What are the odds of ten of your friends seeing something **wrong** with him that you **don't**, and those same ten friends being unable to see the **good** that you **do**?*

Of the two opposing sides, who is more likely to be thinking clearly? Who has no emotional investment in him but deeply cares for you?

But… you want him and nothing anyone says is going to change your mind. Six months later, you're miserable and unable to understand why he suddenly became such a jerk.

The truth is he was always a jerk. You just refused to see it. Or that he's prone to violence, and there are always clues regarding that. Or any number of obvious defects that you plainly refused to acknowledge.

So here's how to resolve that problem.

First, take the time to figure out the type of guy you want. And put considerable thought into this. What you imagine you want, may not be what will make you happy.

Want a rich guy? Most rich guys travel on business and put in long hours. Same goes for professional men, such as doctors and lawyers.

This means you'll be spending a lot of time alone. And if you don't enjoy that, set your sights elsewhere.

Want a strong man who works with his hands? This type often comes home dirty and exhausted. He'll expect his meals to be ready, and his house in order, even if you too have a job.

Love the artistic type? Artistic people are usually a lot of fun to be around. They are also usually poor. And often poor for long periods of time. They work low paying jobs they have no interest in and become miserable hoping that their art or music or photography or whatever catches on and transforms them into rich businessmen.

Sometimes it does. Most times it doesn't. In either case, you can expect to be living in small cheap apartments and watching every nickel for a considerable amount of time.

If you long to be the suburban housewife with the 2.5 kids and a minivan. Then set your sights on a guy who comes from that environment and enjoys it. But if you swoon at the sight of a big, burly biker and figure you can get him AND the suburban lifestyle, you are setting yourself up for a life of misery, disappointment, and unhappiness.

Men and Women Communication Breakdown.

Another important factor to take into consideration is that men don't communicate the same way women do. And this is a constant thorn in the side of most wives. "He never listens to me!" they complain.

Perhaps the problem is that what you're talking about is of no interest to him. Just because it's interesting to you, don't assume that he cares about your Aunt Sadie's sea cruise or your girlfriend's new apartment.

One big misunderstanding between women and men is that women want men to at least make the effort to think like they do.

Again the duck and the horse analogy. Men's brains become activated when it appears it has a job to do. When women tell men their problems, they don't want them to fix it, they just want them to listen. This behavior helps them sort through the problem and resolve it.

The problem here is that when a man's brain realizes it's not needed; it goes into something similar to a computer's sleep mode. So if you just want to talk about your problem and don't want him to think of a way to resolve it, don't bother him with it.

Call a girlfriend and talk to her. Too often women expect men to adopt female traits and become annoyed when they don't.

Men don't expect their wives to lug a 100-pound bag of rock salt out to the driveway, so why do women expect their husbands to get hints?

And women do this all the time. They drop hints that they don't want to date a guy anymore, or want a particular item for their birthday, or are lonely and want someone to talk to and so on.

I don't know a single straight man who has ever understood what his wife is hinting at. This convoluted method of trying to tell her husband what she wants without actually telling him is always a recipe for disappointment and bad feelings.

I understand that women think it's romantic and thoughtful, but men don't get it. Stop setting yourselves up for a let-down and then taking it out on us because you refuse to believe that men don't get hints.

We don't. And once you come to terms with that fact, you'll be a lot happier.

If you want something, tell him, if you need something, tell him, if you feel he's not doing his share of the chores, tell him, if you want him to act in a particular way, tell him.

Just DON'T tell him to act in a way that's completely foreign to what he is. Because he can't and if you're disappointed by that then he's not at fault. You are, because you're the one who made the wrong choice

Another sore point is the wife offering their husband's services. Say your husband is a plumber and your friend mentions that she has a leaky sink. So you casually say, "Oh, no problem. I'll have my husband drop by and have a look at it.

This makes her feel good and helpful.

But let's reverse this scenario. Say one of your husband's friend mentions that his living room carpet is dirty and needs to be cleaned. What if he said, "Oh, no problem. My wife just shampooed the rugs at our house and did a great job! I'll send her right over.

I assume her next job wouldn't be cleaning the friend's rug but cleaning her husband's blood off hers.

***

Here's another fact you need to take into account. And that is:

Every marriage makes its own rules.

And the first thing you need to create and both agree to abide by, is the rules of YOUR marriage. This is so important that I wrote a popular book about those rules titled ***The Best Book on Getting Married*** *featuring the 100 questions you must ask your potential spouse BEFORE tying the knot.*

While researching that book I realized why so many modern marriages wound up in divorce. The reason is because the couple really hadn't taken the time to fully get to know each other, or had presented a persona that they immediately abandoned once they tied the knot.

Another cause of marriages falling apart is when one partner winds up doing all the work while the other finds excuses or is conveniently unavailable when its their turn to do the chores.

That's why it's so important to a happy marriage to decide upon certain rules before exchanging vows.

A happy marriage is one that works for both partners. To some, money is the most important, to others sexual monogamy, having children, starting a business, traveling, socializing, living in the city, living in the country.

It's also important to have similar sexual preferences. Don't pretend to like something you don't, then take that off the table after marriage.

Again that is why it's so important to analyze a possible relationship before committing to one, and yes, I know that's not romantic, it's nothing like those movies, where the man sweeps the woman off her feet that women enjoy so much. It seems cold, analytical and methodical. And nothing that remotely resembles that rush you get with a new romance.

It's almost as powerful a feeling as the utter misery you'll experience when you discover the guy is a habitual liar, cheat, and thief.

It would have taken just a little effort to make some inquiries about him. Have a look at his Facebook page, what does it say about his likes and interests? If he has a blog, what does it say? How long was he with his last girlfriend? What are his hobbies? What do his friends say about him?

What his friends say, (or don't say) will likely be the most valuable bit of information you will get. This is because guys, as much as they like their buddy, are, in most cases, naturally protective of women. So if they hesitate and start looking for metaphors to describe the type of guy he is, what they are doing is trying to be a good friend while at the same time warning you that he's probably not right for you.

This as close as a guy will ever get to giving a hint. If it's not an enthusiastic endorsement set your sights elsewhere.

WHY YOUR JOB CAN MAKE YOU UNHAPPY

Why Feminism is at odds with Femininity

I like Feminism. Why? Because it levels the playing field. The goal of feminism is to ensure that women are treated the same as men in the workplace. That they get the same pay for the same job, get the same benefits and opportunities.

Fair is fair.

The problem is when it comes to treating women the same way you treat men.

Everything seemed to be running along just fine until the 1970's oil embargo hit. Back in those days, men watched their language when around women, they opened doors, pulled out chairs, let them go first, and put them on pedestals. In return, women cooked and cleaned and raised the children.

Then the sudden lack of cheap oil made prices spike dramatically and women were forced to take jobs just so the family could make ends meet.

And so the rules of behavior changed and neither men or women had a clear idea of how to address this new paradigm.

When a man screws up on the job, costs the company money, and slow production, the boss will chew his head off, usually using words not meant for polite society.

Men understand this. We understand that if we screw up we're going to get slammed, HARD.

So we take the verbal beating, lick our wounds and make damn sure we don't that mistake EVER again.

Do that to a woman and the company will be facing multiple lawsuits. And what is so unfair about it is that the jury will always side with the women because they have been programmed since childhood that women are made of sugar and spice and everything nice. They are our mothers and sisters and we, as men, have a genetic need to protect them.

And so they walk away with a wad of cash. Basically a reward for being a screw-up.

And that's not fair. You see, feminism and femininity are mutually exclusive. Meaning you can't have both.

The Japanese view business as war. And all is fair in love and war. And in war you are not allowed to be feminine, to be dainty, to be sensitive. You can't pout because no one noticed your new hairdo or that everyone forgot (most likely didn't care,) that today was your birthday.

This is not to say that a woman can't be as good a boss or as tough a boss as a man. They certainly can as history has proven. My youngest daughter is the CFO of a multimillion dollar company.

And you will never meet a tougher negotiator. When she decided to buy a new car some years ago she asked me to come along because I knew what cars were worth buying and which ones weren't. Certainly not because she needed her 'daddy' to give her confidence.

Because my daughter is slight (5'2" and only a little over 100 lbs.) the salesman obviously saw her as a pushover. So he tried to upsell all kinds of crap, until my daughter had had enough, leaned in and verbally began to rip his head off.

When he turned to me with a look of desperation, I merely smiled. Afterward when she used her forearm to wipe the proverbial blood from her mouth and chin, she leaned back and said, "Now here's what you're going to do."

During my corporate career, I've had a couple of female bosses. And they were just as able and competent as any of my male bosses.

The reality is this. A woman is far more likely to be fired for a mistake than a man. And the reason is that the boss can make a guy feel so miserable for screwing up that he'll never make a mistake like that again.

And he won't.

The boss can't do that to a woman without risking a lawsuit so instead, he finds a way to "Let her go."

This too is unfair.

And this reality is unfair to both men and women. And frankly, I don't know the answer.

You can't expect a woman to simply lose her femininity. It what makes her who she is. But having been in corporate for so many years I understand that business is highly competitive and that sensitivity, nurturing and compassion are viewed as signs of weakness.

And many men still resent having a female boss. They still feel women should be assistants, not bosses.

However, times are changing and this issue regarding women in the workplace may become unimportant because in the future there will be far more successful home based businesses than corporate monoliths.

Here's why.

Advancing technology and outsourcing are making the non-specialist employee obsolete. Computers and the internet are eliminating far more jobs than they are creating.

For example, IBM has created a computer called Watson. It has the capacity to answer any question faster than any human being and to prove it they featured the computer on the game show Jeopardy and it beat the show's most winningest contestants, Ken Jennings, and Brad Rudder.

When it becomes available for purchase, it will eliminate all customer service jobs.

The 3D Printer presently has the capacity to eliminate most assembly-line and manufacturing jobs.

The Google car technology will eliminate most if not all, truck, bus and taxi driving jobs.

If you are a woman with a job, then you already know how precarious the job market is.

You've likely seen friends and co-workers "let go" because of the economic crunch. So to be aware is a good thing. It keeps you sharp and attentive as to what your company needs.

But you also need to be realistic.

Walmart is closing over 250 stores, Sears and K-Mart over 100. Target has had layoffs as have many big box retailers.

Why? Because businesses are transferring their companies to the internet. And with good reason.

I often tell the story about the difference between Walmart and Amazon. Here's how it goes.

While shopping at Walmart I saw a man carefully examining a large flat screen TV box. Then write down its specs. I thought maybe he was going to look it up on Consumers Reports or something.

It wasn't until later when we were both waiting for the rain to stop before heading to our cars when I saw that same man on his cell phone.

I was standing behind him and noticed that he wasn't talking or texting someone.

He was on Amazon ordering the same big screen TV he had looked over in Walmart electronic section earlier.

I also noted the Amazon's price was cheaper and it came with free shipping.

That is why the internet is the future of business. The internet, as well as advancing technology and outsourcing, is making the human employee obsolete.

If you have a job, there is absolutely no guarantee that you will still have one tomorrow. The economy is that volatile. And things are changing that fast.

So what do you do? You do what I did. You start your own online business. It's extremely easy to do and can be very lucrative once you get the hang of it.

I created a website that showing beginners how it's done, what you need to do, and the few products you'll need to get started.

Frankly, I strongly suggest that everyone who reads this book, get an online business.

What's that old saying, Forewarned is forearmed?

One of the most important things a happy woman does is accept her reality. If you're in a retail job, or customer service or manufacturing you need to start seriously considering your future. Those jobs are being phased out.

Want an example? The Walmart in my area originally had 4 automatic cashier stations.

They now have twelve.

To get started with an online business go to http://startanonlinebusiness.info I created that site so anyone looking to increase their income could learn how.

WHO ARE YOU?

Determining Who You Are Is The Key to Becoming A Happy Woman

Depending on your self-image you are likely much better looking than you think or much worse. I spoke earlier of how your brain controls what you see and often what you hear.

And in regards to what you see, it can be dangerously insidious, frightening and life threatening. Few knew or understood anorexia nervosa until Karen Carpenter's condition hit the tabloids.

It simply made no sense. She was losing weight at a frightening rate, causing mountains of physical problems brought on by the lack of nutrients. She was skin and bones and was beginning to look like an Auschwitz victim.

The difference was that Auschwitz prisoners had no say in their emaciated condition. Karen did.

Or so we thought. So why would a beautiful, loving, successful major talent, literally starve herself to death?

Because every time she saw an image of herself either in a mirror or on film or in photos, her brain made her look fat.

Horrifying isn't it. The poor soul was nearly skeletal yet in every mirror a fat girl was looking back at her, in every photo, in every video, she was fat. And getting fatter.

And when you can't believe what you see…

That poor soul never had a chance.

I bring this up to show how important it is to know ourselves and to treat ourselves the way we need to be treated. Psychiatrists now believe that anorexia nervosa patients act this way because of a desperate need to take control over some form of their lives.

And determining the amount of food they consume is one thing they have complete control over and so the brain, ever the faithful servant takes action to make you into the person its thinks you want to be.

Even if it kills you.

Many scientists presently fear the creation of A.I. also known as artificial intelligence. The concern with artificial intelligence (put simply it when a computer becomes smart enough to become self-aware,) the computer may see us as a hindrance because we have the power to turn it on or off, and therefore the ability to kill it. Logically it would be to its advantage to kill us first, and since it doesn't have the higher brain function of our conscious mind, it would have no qualms about doing that.

It is believed our subconscious acts in the same manner.

This is why your attitude is so important. That's why your self-esteem is so important and that why it is so important for you to do whatever is necessary to make yourself happy. Because if you remain unhappy and despondent your subconscious will eventually decide that this is what you want and make you even more so.

So who are you really?

This is very important to discover. Some people are far more sensitive than others. Some far more intelligent, some more vindictive, selfish, sexual, loving, jealous, generous, miserly, there are such a large number of possible combinations that it is hard to figure out who you really are.

One of the biggest mistake we make as people is assuming that others think the same way we do.

The truth is, nobody thinks like you do.

And that is what friends are for. But make sure they are your real friends. I have discovered there are a number of so-called friends who'd like nothing more than to see you fall flat on your face. So choose wisely and whatever they say about you, accept it and make a point not to hold it against them no matter how much it hurts.

Because it's what you NEED to know.

The Great Adventure.

We're all well acquainted with the term middle-age crazy. A term that is almost always applied to older men. This is where the man buys a sleek sports car, gets hair plugs, goes to the gym and tries to get himself back into shape.

Many people assume the old goat is trying to look younger to attract some young honey, but in most cases the reason is because he's beginning to look and feel old and he doesn't want to be viewed as someone who can no longer support and protect his family.

That's male ego for you. Eventually, he succumbs to the reality of his situation and accepts it.

Middle-age crazy for women is something completely different. I call it The Great Adventure.

This usually occurs a few years after menopause has passed and the kids have gone off to college. This is when some women convince themselves that there is a life full of love and adventure waiting for them but they're stuck with a husband they no longer love and dreams to be free of him, so they can finally have all they deserve.

Besides, she's a victim. She raised his children, cooked his meals, took care of his gross sexual needs, kept his house, paid the bills and oh so much more and what did she get in return…

… A dull, lackluster life.

Why she could have been so many things, had so many exciting adventures, met so many interesting people, traveled more, lived more, loved more…

And it isn't too late. She could still have all those things but she has to get out of the marriage first.

And once one partner decides the marriage is over, any attempts by the other partner to keep the marriage alive is viewed as obstruction and victimization.

She can't wait until the divorce is finalized so she can finally start living!

She takes the money from the settlement, rents a small studio apartment and books herself a cruise. And it's fun! She meets new people, sees exciting new places. And when she arrives back all the people she met agree to keep in contact.

But as in all phases of life, these promises to remain in touch peter out, so she joins clubs and takes classes and starts dating. And it's all good. But there are too many nights where she's alone with no one to talk to.

She tries to spend more time with her children but they have become standoffish and blame her for breaking up their family. She begins to feel like the third wheel when invited to dinner parties. Married women eye her as a possible threat.

She longs for companionship and agrees to sex when she would have preferred not to but it's better than spending another night alone.

What she also doesn't know is that the majority of people who contract sexually transmitted diseases are not teens or swinging young singles. By a wide margin it's men and women over fifty because they no longer need to be concerned about getting pregnant, so they don't use protection.

After a few years, her middle-age crazy peters out and she starts to review the whys she felt she needed to leave her husband. Starts to seriously reevaluate her reasoning and her supposed victimhood.

Yes, she raised his children but they were her children too.

Yes, she cooked his meals but she was cooking for herself and the kids so adding another plate was no great sacrifice.

Yes, she took care of his sexual needs but to be honest, she enjoyed it as much as he did.

Yes, she kept the house but she kept it the way she wanted it. All the furniture and fixtures were of her choosing. Everything except the big screen TV and the recliner.

And yes, she paid the bills but he made the majority of the money and faithfully turned it over to her to spend as she saw fit.

And he wasn't a bad husband, yes a bit dull at times, but he never beat her, never strayed, always had a job, and he did love her and was clearly devastated when she announced she wanted a divorce.

Then she thinks that perhaps she made a mistake. True, she did a few things she likely never would have done had she remained married but to be honest, they weren't all that terrific.

The pyramids don't look all that different in real life than they do on TV. Traveling was fun but too much and too long becomes wearisome. And yes, the sex was exciting at first, but the men who found her attractive weren't interested in a relationship and after a while she began feeling used.

She starts to make inquires as to what her ex-husband is up to. Maybe there is a possibility of rekindling their romance…

But she learns that her husband has recently remarried because older men don't like living alone.

She had not been told of or invited to the wedding. When she asked her daughter why, she replied, "I didn't think you'd care. Besides, it's not like you're a member of the family anymore."

Those words stung but she had to admit they were true. Her children stayed with her ex during summer vacations and spring breaks. While she was having her great adventure he was home and available whenever the kids needed him.

My research taught me this. More times than not, older women who divorced their husbands to go on their great adventure later regretted it. They saw only the adventure, not the cost. And the cost was the banishment of all the shared memories created over a lifetime of marriage.

The anniversary celebrations, gone.

The holiday vacation albums, gone.

The in-jokes, and shared adventures gone.

The intimacy, gone.

The trust, gone.

The extended family, gone.

The marriage album or video, gone.

The wedding and engagement rings, gone.

A near lifetime of shared hopes and dreams and accomplishments and failures now looked back upon with sorrow because of its terrible ending.

Of course, there are those women who couldn't be happier living the single life again.

As mentioned throughout this book, happiness greatly depends on the decisions we make. And once we chose, we must accept the ramifications. No one is going to swoop in and make it all better. No amount of tears, pleading and I'm sorrys will erase the events our decisions create.

Emotions come and go, but cold logic and reason win in the long run every time.

So as much as one would like to believe, there is no Prince Charming, no royal ball, no majestic castle, no rescue from the tower, and no guaranteed happy ever after.

It's just you and you alone who decides your fate. Others are not put here to make you happy. You decide to do whatever is necessary to make yourself happy or you don't.

FINAL NOTES

I will assume there were parts of this book where you snarled and said, "This guy is an insensitive jerk, as well as parts where you probably said, "Aw crap, he's right."

And the reason I felt so confident that I would be a better able to teach you how to become a happy woman, than some touchy-feely, hand holding female author is because I am a happy man.

And I became a happy man by doing everything I taught you in this book. And when it comes down to reality, both men and women aren't all that different. We have to face our lives and our shortcomings the same way in order to correct them. We have to take responsibility for our actions and if we want our lives to change, then we have to change ourselves.

The most important parts to remember is that YOU PROGRAM YOUR BRAIN. Whatever you tell yourself you are, you subconscious will try to make that happen.

Understand the difference between a must and a should. You will never succeed when you tell yourself you SHOULD do something. You will only succeed when you MUST do something.

Understand that you will fail far more often than you will succeed. We learn by failing, success is a poor teacher. But the difference between a happy person and a sad person is that a happy person corrects their mistakes and programs themselves not to make those mistakes again.

Understand that in order to be happy, you need to be constantly improving yourself. Discover what you're interested in and learn more about it. Learn enough and you could write a book about it. Sell it online.

That's what I do.

Remember to ask yourself, "What job would I do even if I wasn't getting paid for it?" Because that will show you who you really are and what you're really meant to do.

And lastly, I want you to succeed. The reason I succeeded in becoming a happy man is because I allowed myself to become so miserable that I had no choice. And I credit Dr. Fuhrman's infomercial with showing me that, by making the necessary changes, I could dramatically improve my life.

I also credit Tony Robbins with showing me how to change my negative thinking and reinforcing the importance of making each action a must instead of a should.

And I want to thank Robert Kiyosaki for teaching me how the financial industry works and how to increase my income by smart investing.

But most importantly, I want to thank you for buying this book, and I sincerely hope that it has helped and put you on a mission to self-improvement and happiness.

And if so please write a review and tell those who may also need to know what you and I have learned.

Disclaimer

How to Become a Happy Woman is a self-improvement book and is not intended to be a medical text. If you suffer from depression or suicidal thoughts, you need to contact a medical professional as this book will be of no help to you.

The author is not a medical professional nor is he a therapist or psychologist.

This book is copyrighted 2016 by Zackary Richards and published by Ari Publishing.

The Ari Publishing star logo is copyrighted and is the sole property of Ari Communications and cannot be duplicated or used to promote any product not related to Ari Communications or its subsidiaries.

No portion of this book may be reproduced in any fashion without the written consent of the author.

To view other books by this author, go to:

http://zackaryrichards.com

www.ingramcontent.com/pod-product-compliance
Lightning Source LLC
Chambersburg PA
CBHW071300040426
42444CB00009B/1807